I0107912

Easter

The World's Best News

William Lyon Phelps

✝✝✝

Copyright © 2013 Read Books Ltd.
This book is copyright and may not be
reproduced or copied in any way without
the express permission of the publisher in writing

British Library Cataloguing-in-Publication Data
A catalogue record for this book is available from the
British Library

William Lyon Phelps

William Lyon Phelps was born on 2nd January 1865, in New Haven, Conneticut, United States.

Phelps earned a B.A. in 1887, writing his thesis on the Idealism of George Berkeley. He then gained an M.A. in 1891 from Yale and his PhD from Harvard in the same year. During his time a Yale, he offered a course in modern novels which brought the university considerable attention both nationally and internationally. This was quite controversial at the time and Phelps was pressured to give up the course, but eventually, due to popular demand, reinstated it outside the official curriculum.

In 1892, Phelps married Annabel Hubbard, sister of childhood friend Frank Hubbard, and the couple moved to the family estate overlooking Lake Huron. Phelps christened it "The House of the Seven Gables", after the Nathanial Hawthorne story of the same name.

He became a very popular figure at Yale but also as an

inspirational orator. He went on lecture tours that drew large audiences, speaking on the virtues of modern literature. He also preached regularly at the Huron City Methodist Episcopal Church and attracted such large crowds that the church was remodelled twice in five years to accommodate them.

Phelps published many essays on modern and European literature, including titles such as *Essays on Modern Novelists* (1910), *Some Makers of American Literature* (1923), and *As I Like it* (1923).

After his retirement from Yale in 1933, after 41 years of service, Phelps continued his public speaking, preaching, and writing a newspaper column. He also sat on book selection committees and acted as a judge for the Pulitzer Prize for literature.

His wife, Annabel, died from a stroke in 1939 and Phelps died four years later, in 1943.

CONTENTS

THE WORLD'S BEST NEWS

I

THE WORLD'S
BEST NEWS

IF YOU wish absolute accuracy, do not say "Easter Sunday." Say either Easter or Easter Day. The Sunday is included in the word; and to say Easter Sunday is really like saying Thanksgiving Thursday.

A fairly common surname in English is *Lovejoy*. No name is more Christian in its origin and significance. The two syllables are the keynotes of the Christian religion; they naturally go together, for the first

begets the second. In musical par-
lance, the first chord is a suspension,
the second a solution.

I come of strictly Puritan stock,
and am glad of it. But it is difficult to
forgive the Puritans for taking de-
light and mirth out of the practice
of religion.

In a famous play by Strindberg,
the Baptist aunt said to the unbe-
lieving captain, "Why don't you
believe in the love of God?" and the
captain replied, "Look here, Auntie,
why is it that whenever you speak of
the love of God, you look so hateful?
A positively venomous expression
comes into your eyes. No, Auntie,
you have not got the true faith." She

was a bad advertisement of religion.

Life is serious. Such was the motto
of Carlyle's *Past and Present*—"*Ernst
ist das Leben.*" The Christian lives in
eternity, and the strength of his
sympathy for humanity makes his
heart ache at the enormous amount
of suffering, poverty, wickedness, and
cruelty in the world. But, perhaps,
this very darkness makes the Light
shine all the more brightly; surely the
Light is not superfluous. In the difficult part of life, we need the Light;
and it is encouraging to remember
that the adverse winds of nineteen
centuries have not been able to
extinguish it.

The two great *feasts* of the Christian

religion are Christmas and Easter—
both days of joy. They are celebrated
to-day by more people than at any
previous time. The Incarnation and
the Resurrection make the best news
the world has ever received.

It is fortunate that both of these
tremendous ideas are within the
understanding of a little child, and
can not be outgrown by the wisest
years of intellectual maturity. For
the four Gospels in which they are
contained constitute a masterpiece of
literature, outshining in sheer excel-
lence the best works of Shakespeare
and Homer.

THE FEAR OF DEATH

II

THE FEAR OF DEATH

TO ATTAIN eminence in the law or in medicine or in engineering, one must give one's mind to years of assiduous study; merely to converse intelligently with Einstein requires almost a life-time of mathematical research. But one does not have to attend a university or pursue learning in a graduate school to obtain the secret of Christianity; sometimes its secret is hidden from the wise and prudent, and revealed unto babes; even as the least in the kingdom of Heaven is greater than the most brilliant citizen of any other kingdom.

All men and women who are fighters, whether they fight foes without or more insidious foes within, realize the supreme sweetness of victory. Victory is always the goal of battle. No matter what the personal qualities of a commander may be, if he lead his soldiers to victory after victory, he will receive their unquestioning adoration. We know how hundreds of thousands of Frenchmen followed wherever Napoleon chose to go. We know that when he returned almost alone from Elba, and the armed forces of the kingdom went out to crush him, he said, "Soldiers, it is the Emperor!" and they left all and followed him. The thrilling song "Two Grenadiers" expresses the deathless devotion of the Old Guard. Even to-day, after the lapse of more than a century, it is impossible to read of Napoleon or to think of him without feeling his spell.

But of all the leaders of men of whom we have any record, Our Lord stands immeasurably first. No other was ever so independent, so free from fear, so indifferent to consequences. As He was never afraid of any earthly power or potentate or of the hostility of organized public opinion, so He feared neither life nor death. The great dramatist Ibsen, after he had attained the height of his ambition, said it took more courage to live than to die. On the other hand, Doctor Johnson, who showed unflinching courage in daily life, had the icy sweat of fear whenever he thought of death.

THE JOY OF VICTORY

III

THE JOY OF VICTORY

OUR Lord never minimized life's tragedies. But He said "Be of good cheer: I have overcome the world." It will be well if we remember in the hours of despondency that we follow a Conqueror; who in the midst of turbulence remained inwardly serene. In the trial before Pilate, He was the only person in the hall who was wholly calm.

Easter celebrates His final and most decisive victory, when the King of Terrors was defeated by the King of Kings. He had given an illustration of His power over death in the resurrection of Lazarus. No event recorded in the New Testament, with the two exceptions of the birth and death of Jesus himself, has had a greater germinal effect on literature than Lazarus. It is the inspiration of innumerable stories, poems, and plays. But until Browning wrote his poem on the Strange Medical Experience of Karhsish, novelists and poets had missed the supreme significance of the story. They had all concentrated their attention on those veiled days in the tomb—where was Lazarus then, was he conscious, what did he see beyond the bourne?

Browning is not interested in that at all. The question he asks is not what happened to Lazarus in the tomb, but what effect did that experience have on his character? Was Lazarus exactly the same man he had been before his rehearsal of death? For, just as there are people who hear sublime music, have amazing adventures, and see the wonders of the world, without any resulting change in themselves, so there are others whose characters are transformed by one experience.

Such was Browning's Lazarus. He was spiritually reborn, his whole scale of values reversed. Eugene O'Neill, in his drama, *Lazarus Laughed*, has consciously or unconsciously followed in the wake of Browning.

For, if we do not profit by experience, we are as well off without it.

The Christian Church is founded on Easter. It is pleasant to see the whole world rejoicing. Even what the newspapers call the Easter Parade of fashion has its peculiar grace. Men and women put on shining sartorial uniforms and walk in the sunlight. The former resplendence of the "Easter Bonnet" had a certain charm. If ever there was an occasion for the display of glittering apparel, it is Easter. We are celebrating a victory infinitely greater and more far-reaching than that of Armistice Day.

I happened to attend Easter service in a Catholic Church in Augusta; the priest remarked in his sermon, "If Christ did not rise from the dead, the Catholic Church would be the greatest enigma in all human history." And so it would.

Something tremendous happened. The disciples had deserted him on the only occasion when He really felt a need of them. Their high hopes of the coming kingdom were shattered; their leader, after all his confident talk, actually died; and died the ignominious and horrible death of a miserable criminal, accompanied in His last agony by two common thieves.

Then, on the third day, came sun-
rise—the most magnificent dawn
humanity has known. The formerly
despairing and scattered disciples re-
united in triumph. No more doubt,
no more questioning, no more un-
certainty, no more gloom. The early
apostolic days were marked by a
confidence which nothing could dim.
Out of their joyous triumphant *certainty* came the Christian Church.
Never was there in any assemblage
a more complete transformation—it
was the change from utter and
apparently hopeless defeat to the
obstreperous joy of victory.

THE GREATEST GIFT

IV

THE GREATEST GIFT

T IS not my purpose to argue about the Resurrection. But to those who wish to read on that aspect of the question, I will recommend two books—*According to Saint John*, by Lord Charnwood, and *Who Moved the Stone?* by Frank Morison. Lord Charnwood is a professional biographer; he is the author of the best one-volume Life of Lincoln. He began the study of the Fourth Gospel with an open mind; applying the same methods and tests that he would use in any serious work of historical or biographical investigation. In his own words, he emerged from this study "an ordinary Christian." Frank Morison, another Englishman, investigated the story of "the empty tomb" in the legal style of a search for evidence; he tells the results in a manner that gains in impressiveness by the absence of sentiment.

There is more and better evidence for the Resurrection than for any other miracle. It is encouraging to remember that the story is told in all four Gospels, and that it was the foundation as well as the inspiration of the whole career of St. Paul.

But the most important fact is,

and will be, its direct effect on our own spiritual lives. We cannot live richly and fully, and certainly not hopefully and joyously, without the mystery of the Unknown, without the thought of something beyond our earthly existence. Browning, in his poem, *Easter Day*, imagines himself for a moment offered the gift by God of continuous and eternal life in this world with good health and good mental powers, with everything we ask for day by day—only, with the certainty that this is all—no mysterious future, no hope beyond this pleasant routine. The thought becomes unendurable.

We read occasionally of someone

who, after long struggles with sordid
poverty, was made rich overnight by
some unsuspected will. He enters
joyfully upon his inheritance. Well,
as the Word made Flesh is the
greatest gift man has ever received,
we should not cower or shrink, but
stand up and walk abroad like free
men and women, rejoicing in our
inheritance, fearless and unafraid.

No Christian ever has to explain
God. The nature of the Supreme
Energy we can not define. All our
faith, all our hopes, are based on One
Person. If He rose from the grave,
we hope to be with Him in Paradise.
If He died and mouldered in decay
and ruin, that is what we ask for

ourselves. For wherever He is, that is
where we want to be.

"LET ME GO ON!"

"LET ME GO ON!"

"Love is the best? 'T is somewhat late!
  And all thou dost enumerate
Of power and beauty in the world,
  The mightiness of love was curled
Inextricably round about
  Love lay within it and without,
To clasp thee,—but in vain! Thy soul
  Still shrunk from Him who made the whole,
Still set deliberate aside
  His love!—Now take love! Well betide
Thy tardy conscience! Haste to take
  The show of love for the name's sake,
Remembering every moment Who,
  Beside creating thee unto
These ends, and these for thee, was said
  To undergo death in thy stead
In flesh like thine: so ran the tale.
  What doubt in thee could countervail
Belief in it? Upon the ground
  'That in the story had been found
Too much love! How could God love so?'
  He who in all his works below
Adapted to the needs of man,
  Made love the basis of the plan,—
Did love, as was demonstrated:
  While man, who was so fit instead
To hate, as every day gave proof,—
  Man thought man, for this kind's behoof,
Both could and did invent that scheme

Of perfect love: 't would well beseem
Cain's nature thou wast wont to praise,
Not tally with God's usual ways!"

And I cowered deprecatingly—
    "Thou Love of God! Or let me die,
Or grant what shall seem heaven almost!
    Let me not know that all is lost,
Though lost it be—leave me not tied
    To this despair, this corpse-like bride!
Let that old life seem mine—no more—
    With limitation as before,
With darkness, hunger, toil, distress:
    Be all the earth a wilderness!
Only let me go on, go on,
    Still hoping ever and anon
To reach one eve the Better Land!"
    Then did the form expand, expand—
I knew Him through the dread disguise
    As the whole God within His eyes
Embraced me. When I lived again,
    The day was breaking,—the gray plain
I rose from, silvered thick with dew.
    Was this a vision? False or true?
Since then, three varied years are spent,
    And commonly my mind is bent
To think it was a dream—be sure
    A mere dream and distemperature—
The last day's watching: then the night,—
    The shock of that strange Northern Light
Set my head swimming, bred in me
    A dream. And so I live, you see,

Go through the world, try, prove, reject,
    Prefer, still struggling to effect
My warfare; happy that I can
    Be crossed and thwarted as a man,
Not left in God's contempt apart,
    With ghastly smooth life, dead at heart,
Tame in earth's paddock as her prize.
Thank God, she still each method tries
To catch me, who may yet escape,
    She knows,—the fiend in angel's shape!
Thank God, no paradise stands barred
    To entry, and I find it hard
To be a Christian, as I said!
    Still every now and then my head
Raised glad, sinks mournful—all grows drear
    Spite of the sunshine, while I fear
And think, 'How dreadful to be grudged
    No ease henceforth, as one that 's judged.
Condemned to earth forever, shut
    From heaven!' But Easter Day breaks! But
Christ rises! Mercy every way
    Is infinite,—and who can say?"

—From Robert Browning's *Easter Day*

www.ingramcontent.com/pod-product-compliance
Lightning Source LLC
Chambersburg PA
CBHW051741040426
42447CB00008B/1251